The Beautiful ᴸ

To the memory of Lady Jane Franklin,
who never read novels but knew how to make heroes.

The Beautiful Lie
Sheenagh Pugh

seren

Seren is the book imprint of
Poetry Wales Press Ltd
Nolton Street, Bridgend, Wales
www.seren-books.com

ISBN 1-85411-311-9

A CIP record for this title is available from
the British Library

The publisher works with the financial assistance of the
Arts Council of Wales

Cover Image: *Risky Game in Disko Bay* (detail),
Michael Vogeley, *www.michael-vogeley.de*

Printed in Palatino by
Bell & Bain Ltd, Glasgow

Contents

The Beautiful Lie

He was about four, I think... it was so long ago.
In a garden; he'd done some damage
behind a bright screen of sweet-peas
– snapped a stalk, a stake, I don't recall,
but the grandmother came and saw, and asked him:
"Did you do that?"

Now, if she'd said *why* did you do that,
he'd never have denied it. She showed him
he had a choice. I could see in his face
the new sense, the possible. That word and deed
need not match, that you could say the world
different, to suit you.

When he said "No", I swear it was as moving
as the first time a baby's fist clenches
on a finger, as momentous as the first
taste of fruit. I could feel his eyes looking
through a new window, at a world whose form
and colour weren't fixed

but fluid, that poured like a snake, trembled
around the edges like northern lights, shape-shifted
at the spell of a voice. I could sense him filling
like a glass, hear the unreal sea in his ears.
This is how to make songs, create men, paint pictures,
tell a story.

I think I made up the screen of sweet-peas.
Maybe they were beans; maybe there was no screen:
it just felt as if there should be, somehow.
And he was my – no, I don't need to tell that.
I know I made up the screen. And I recall very well
what he had done.

The Lit Room

i.m. George Mackay Brown

There was a flat
on a long street by the sea,
a room, scarcely lit,

a head of clay,
sunken-eyed, cheekbones hollowed,
a *memento mori*

for the face that glowed
from the shadows, so gaunt, so mobile.
There was a word

someone let fall,
that filled him, all of a sudden,
with light. A vessel

of ware so thin,
the wine shone through. Light leaks
into the ocean

when the clay cracks,
into the dark. Who notices
if the street lacks

one lamp, one face?
These days, the room is empty
of shadows,

well-lit, tidy.
There is a flat, on a long street
by the sea...

FANFIC

Fanfic is a sequence of poems about the interface between fiction and reality, and how fictional characters acquire a degree of reality via their fans' belief in them. It is set in the world of fan fiction and the notes at the end of the sequence are for those to whom the vocabulary of that world is unfamiliar.

I.
Creator

They weren't mine for long. They began
as shapes in my head, yes: the jester,
the idealist, the cynic, the rest,
and I was the first to colour in

patches of them. Then a casting director
gave them bodies, faces. A wardrobe mistress
dressed them. When I heard their voices,
I knew I'd lost them. Though the actors

were what I'd seen, they had eyes too,
and minds to shape with. In a matter
of months, they were saying: "He wouldn't do that".
It wasn't such a wrench to let go,

hand over to the scriptwriters. I'd watch
for each one's angle on them; a new facet
lit up each time. I didn't always like it,
but they weren't mine to dislike. They'd grown so much,

I hardly knew them. When in the end
I disowned them, sure they'd gone astray,
there were plenty who thought differently.
One told me: "They did what was in your mind,

became the enemy, turned into what
they hated, and you meant that to happen
from the day you wrote Episode One:
you just didn't like it when you saw it".

I think that was the cynic... or the jester...
or the man who played him. All I really know
is they were mine, and I lost them somehow,
as soon as I put them down on paper.

2.
The Man I Mean

The man in black and silver
stole millions, killed casually,
kept his word,

threw the best lines away
with a half-smile, faded
in a last-scene shoot-out.

He can still be found
on the Net: the man, I mean,
who never lived:

he's a cult now. Sites
from here to Australia
keep him alive,

the actor, too.
That might be the best place
to look for him

– the actor, I mean –
rather than search
the updated site

of middle age,
its changing face,
for the man's eyes. Some say

he didn't update
– the actor, I mean –
came to believe

in the man: wrote his life,
couldn't move on.
Small blame to him.

Who would let go
of the best time,
the man inside,

if a videotape
could keep his voice,
his spare frame,

if you could scan him
on to a homepage,
download him just

as he was: will be,
the man you still mean
when you say *me*?

3.
A Life

She bloody worries me, I tell you –
talk about obsessive. I recall

when it ended, she said:
"It's like losing your friends".

But Christ, if a friend dies, you grieve
at the funeral, then move on:

you don't set up websites to chat
about them, write bits of their life

that never happened, go to conventions,
watch endless videos.... There's an end

to everything real, but not those bastards
who never lived; they can last

as long as someone writes them. Jealous
of nothing, that's me. What sort of fool,

eh? I'd sooner it was a man,
straight up: I'd feel less lonely.

I'm not stupid. I know she does this
because she feels something's missing:

just don't know what. If I did,
it might not help. What do kids say

these days – get a life? The thing is,
I think that's what she's doing.

4.

Fanfic

This game is old. Listen
to a story – Robin Hood, maybe,
all in the greenwood.

Toy figures become outlaws.
Nottingham Castle grows
from Lego, turns into Camelot,

a Batcave, a flight deck,
and the words are made flesh
over and over.

But stories end
and most children
put their toys away.

This game comes next. Some
never learn it. Run out
of stories: make more stories.

Take the plastic men
and paint their features
with grief, plans, memories.

Whatever you can think,
they can do. The storyteller
can close his spell-book:

you're time-served now: you know
the magic words.
You have the con.

5.
Mary-Sue

I'm going in. I'm armed
with a mind as lethal

as a thermal lance. I hug
the gun close to my side,

my dance partner. I'm dangerous,
but worth it. When I've zapped

his captors, wiped the virus
from his computer, when the guards

are down, I can be gentle,
if gentle's what he wants:

he only needs to look past
my perfect face, my body

laserbeam-straight, taut with youth,
and I'll be there.

And what if every mirror,
every calendar and CV,

every pair of scales
in the world says different,

if all I have is the gift
to see myself as others

don't see me, in a shape,
a world, that never was,

and write it down? It works,
my teleport. I'm going in.

6.
H/c

I don't know why I like watching you suffer,
I really don't. I'm not like that:
you have to know. I couldn't hurt a –
well, I could; I swat them all summer,
but not a man. I couldn't hurt a man,
nor even stand by and see it done.

When I go Net-hunting for h/c,
when I write the stuff, make those things happen
to you: the torture, the slash-rape,
the grief and guilt, I think what hooks me
is knowing I can help. I feel the hurt
for you, holding back the comfort

as long as I can bear to, because I know
it's certain in the end. Every day
I see hurt, read it in the paper
and know it won't stop, whatever I do.
The child in Tesco with his shouting mother
will get hit again, over and over,

– even more, if I try to stop her.
A dancing bear shuffles painfully,
and in some cell the electrodes are ready;
the man shrinks. I put cheques in envelopes,
turn the page, change channels, walk on.
No, I don't stand by and see it done:

I haven't got the guts. I close my eyes.
But I still want the warm rush of caring,
of feeling pity. Pardon me in this thing,
that your non-existent hurt is what I use
for my comfort, as if someone could suffer
for the world and make it right. As if.

7.
Actor

I spoke his words for him. He used my face,
my hands, my voice, to become who he is,

and it isn't this. What they're writing
out there, on the Net, in fanzines,

that isn't him. I can't believe the words
they give him, what they make him go through,

a man so guarded and apart. I feel
as hurt as he would, reading it.

There've been times, I was offered work
I wouldn't take, because it felt wrong

for him. I won't make him act
against his nature. Can't they see

it's the same for me? Defend free speech
all you want: when you come down to it,

I walk about behind that man's eyes.
How can I see those stories and not mind?

And I know what they say. It isn't true.
I know who he is, and who I am,

and I don't confuse them. How could I,
when we're so unlike? I just want the man

not to vanish under this papier-mâché
of lies, reshaped, betrayed

again. He has a right to be seen
as he really is.

8.
IDIC

Yes, it's your face – was –
but you don't own it
any more.

It's part of him now,
like the concept,
the scriptwriters' quips,

the leather gear
from Wardrobe. He's an ocean,
still filling up

from streams and sources
like my fancy. Did you think
it could stop?

Don't fear for him:
he's not some bubble,
colours shifting

in a skin of water
that can thin and break,
shattering brightness.

What the sea can't hold
it throws back out,
and so it is

with his kind. A man of story
accretes, rejects,
comes more alive

with each new teller
of tales. You helped to make
what could outgrow you,

live in the mind's
limitless ways,
but you have to let go.

Gain weight now, go grey:
he won't. When your eyes
grow veined and milky,

his will be bright.
You spoke for him, but when
your voice stops

it will be his
alone. What he can't use
of you will lie

at the high-water mark,
while the light plays
on his fine-boned face,

his lithe movements.
"And if gods had feelings,
they too would grow old.""

˙Li Po: 791-817

19

9.
Alternate

Well, she was tired, I suppose;
she'd been up watching videos till late

and she wasn't really interested,
but I nuzzled, made a pest

of myself, and she played along,
sleepily. No spark, but I needed

the closeness. I'll take what's on offer,
these days. Then she goes all soft

suddenly, relaxes, kisses back,
and I miss a breath. But she's looking

past me somehow, and I know
the look: I know what she's doing.

She's making a *what if*, rewriting
the script. This man, not that...

and she moves like water, and it's perfect,
except it's all for him. I hold her,

not speaking, because it's not my voice
that belongs with this. I'd only

spoil it for her. I let him come
in my body, pulsing, foaming,

eyes full of stars. Then I turn and lie
facing away, because I'm crying.

10.
Filksong

to the tune of "John Riley"

"Woman in the garden walking,
Looking always at the sky,
Why, my love, have you turned from me?"
This then, sirs, was her reply:

"You know what is my true love's name.
He is a constant voyager.
Twenty years now he's been gone,
Still I think to see him here."

"Your love, he fell with gun in hand,
Or died in prison painfully.
He never will return again,
Then, my love, turn back to me."

"If he fell with gun in hand,
Or died in prison painfully,
Why then he cannot live again,
Unless I'm true to his memory."

"Your love, he spoke with others' words,
Nothing of him was his own.
Like a glove without a hand,
Such men die when their story's done."

"If my hand can help him be,
I can write as others can.
While I make him speak and move,
He can live, my story-man."

"Your love, he neither lived nor died.
He is a shape made all of light.
He has no arms to keep you warm,
He cannot comfort you at night."

"If my love's made all of light,
I wish my flesh would set me free,
To float and spin like dust in sunbeams,
That as he is, so I might be.

You know what is my true love's name.
He is a constant voyager.
Twenty years now he's been gone,
Still I think to see him here...."

11.
Missing Scenes

She knows at once the spaces
where stories grow. The chance mention
of some frontier planet,

or a lost love. Something unresolved.
Five days a man spends off-camera.
Whatever happens

out of sight, implied in a glance,
she can fill the gap. She sees them
everywhere now,

the missing scenes; she can't read
a book or watch a film
without shaping sequels,

nor leave a man or woman
a corner of shadow
or a blank page.

That day off sick, the week
away on business; who knows?
What couldn't you do

in three years at college, twenty
in a crap job, a fortnight's
escape each summer?

When she thinks, these days,
of her life, it seems to be
all missing scenes

where something should have happened,
but when she looks for the stories,
they won't come.

12.
Cross-Reality

If she can Mary-Sue into his world,
can he to hers? She likes to fancy

how it would happen. The co-ordinates
screw up, land him in Tesco Metro

by the clingfilm... would he be wearing
that sprayed-on leather suit? Somehow

she's the only one who knows him,
lost in her world, trying not to look it.

She takes his hand, finds him a quiet spot
in the car park, gets a dark-eyed smile

as his outline dissolves into light.
She goes home with his imprint on her eyes.

There'd need to be some fissure, she supposes,
in the fabric of time, some spark

jumping the tracks from one universe
to its parallel... would lightning do it?

But her favourite theory is simply
that if she believes in him enough,

belief will call him like a gravitational pull
across realities, harden his edges

– made of words and light as he is –
into flesh she can touch without a doubt.

If electronic signals add up to a picture
on a screen, then why not stories, images

from many minds to a man? What is belief
but the need for something to be true?

If she waits long enough, he will stand before her,
and she will tell him: *Our waiting brought you.*

13.
Lost

She is searching all the worlds:
Lycos, GoTo, AltaVista,

for his planetfalls, sites
with traces of him.

She lights, sparrowlike, on crumbs
of fact: a grainy picture, a quote,

now and then his voice on tape,
the icy purr that undoes her.

She gives herself time to taste
the shiver, then jerks her thumb

to jump to the next link.
She trawls a virtual bookshelf

for transcripts: each episode
of his life is out there, if you know

where to look, and she knows.
There is always one link further,

another angle, someone else writing
a novel treatment, a sequel

to the final series.... The web
won't let him die, but where is he?

A suit, a screenplay, an actor's voice,
a memory, a spin-off in the minds

that won't let go, that want him
young and travelling for ever.

Sometimes she senses no limit
to him, no end to his story.

The actor, earthbound, has long worn
new suits, new skins. She avoids

all sight of him. It's not him,
the lost young man, any more

than the shape she lives in now
is the one she knows

from old photographs. It's all
out there somewhere. Armed

with her Favorites file, she shortcuts
cyberforests, questions the masters

of knowledge, forgets to eat.
She is tired: her eyes hurt: she scrolls on.

Notes to Fanfic

Alternate: Fanfic (q.v.) story which postulates an alternative to something that happened in the source. E.g. Cathy marries Heathcliff; Avon doesn't shoot Blake on Gauda Prime.

Cross-reality: (also *crossover: cross-universe*). Genre of fanfic (q.v.) which mixes characters from different fictions, (Princess Leia meets Dracula), or fictional characters and real life.

Fanfic: a.k.a. *fan fiction.* Stories about fictional characters from TV, film, novels, etc., written by fans of those characters, for love rather than profit; found in fanzines and on the Net.

Filksong: a.k.a. *filk.* Song on a fanfic theme, usually set to an existing tune. Named by analogy with "folksong"; said to derive from a mistype at an SF convention.

H/c: abbreviation for "hurt/comfort". Fanfic scenario where the hero undergoes intense suffering (physical, emotional or both) before being rescued/consoled by either another character or a Mary-Sue (q.v.).

IDIC: "Infinite Diversity in Infinite Combinations". Star Trek (Vulcan) slogan advocating universal tolerance. Used by fanfic writers to mean, more or less, "everyone should be free to interpret the source material however they want." Producers of source material tend to disagree.

Mary-Sue: Fanfic story where the female lead is not a character from the series/film/whatever, but represents the author. A *Mary-Sue* will do whatever the author herself aspires to – zap the villains, save the galaxy, get off with the hero.

Missing Scene: Fanfic story which fills in a gap in the original where information was withheld or not spelled out.

Slash: a.k.a. "/". Fanfic genre involving two characters (usually male) in a gay relationship. (The 'slash' is the forward slash on a keyboard, linking two names.)

Making Contact

Some sailor-artist sketched it as it happened:
two ships anchored off a new shore,
the Inuit waiting, intrigued, up the beach,
Parry and Ross, backed by a small party
discreetly armed, stepping forward in friendship
to offer the chief (or the foremost idler,
for all they know) their age-old token
of peace the world over: an olive branch.

Parry is holding it out, his metaphor,
and getting nowhere; nobody seems to want
the other end. But Ross is looking round,
taking in a landscape bare of green
to the paper's edge, knowing not a bush
nor tree has ever grown there, and you can see
he's going to turn, any moment, to Parry:
Edward, we might need to rethink this one.

And then they'll give presents, arrive
at an understanding. Parry will write, later,
of thieving primitives with depraved morals.
He himself will be handed down in story
as the idiot who couldn't build a snow house,
didn't know that food was for sharing,
nor how to accept graciously the loan
of a wife.

But for now, for this moment
while he prods the chill air with his olive
and stares into polite blank eyes,
while gestures fall flat and words translate
into gibberish, his helpless shrug mirrors
the other's rueful grin. Reaching out,
missing, balked, wordless, they will never be
so close again.

Elegy

for the books lost in the fire at Canton Library, Cardiff, 1997

William Thomas, schoolmaster, your voice,
those catty, irascible, eighteenth-century diaries
where your neighbours lived on, ears burning;
                                        you'd have known
what he was, the malignant dullard whose only light
came from his matches: you'd have called him a "crot".

Barbara Palmer her life: kings and rope-dancers,
money and love scattering like light,
there's more where that came from, nightly invading
Pepys' delighted dreams: you chose some cads,
but never one without any wit.

The red *Handmaid*, banned from reading tales,
writing her own. Milton: *as good kill
a man, as a good book*, knowing that words
are the witness to our share in reason,
that to hate words is to hate the light.

Worldmakers, manmakers, more god than God,
your creatures live for ever; you can shape
Troy or Ankh-Morpork; you light the clay.
You could make that clod, if you had a mind to,
but he, having none, could make nothing.

He'd only come to steal the computers,
waiting for a getaway van
that never showed. So why set light
to the building – frustration, pique,
tedium, something else he couldn't spell?

I think he stood there, sensing all around
the voices of thought and fancy, the fluent voices
of folk who could string sentences together,
and dimly he felt light crowding in,
threatening, defining his limits,

so he got rid of it: lit a fire
to put out light. Weeks later, workmen
in the blackened shell are still coughing ash,
while the old folk hang round the door,
thinking of warmth, gossip, newspapers.

May he end up in hell, seeing nothing
but your names in print, hearing only words
of grace and wisdom, the glittering spell
of your grammar, knowing his own measure,
charred, shrivelled, eyes burned out with light.

Going to Liverpool

I am a middle-aged woman
travelling on business
and I'm going to Liverpool,

where I'll take time out
to visit Albert Dock
and the museum

where my youth is preserved.
The fashions I followed,
the songs I knew by heart,

the faces that convulsed
my own into screams
and sobs, they'll all be there.

I'm going to Liverpool,
and it is autumn.
The fields outside Leominster

lie in stubble; the leaves
of Ludlow's trees are jaundiced
and flushed with the fever

that says they're finished.
The ticket collector
said, *Thank you, Madam.*

My daughter's grown up
and my mother's dead,
and between the pages

of the notebook
where I'm writing this
I keep a yellowed ticket

to a match, a picture
of an actor, Edwin Morgan's reply
to my fan letter,

and I'm going to Liverpool
because I'm the kind
that always will.

The Boy with a Cloud in his Hand

He hasn't got much: not a roof,
nor a job, nor any great hopes,
but he's got a cloud in his hand
and he thinks he might squeeze
till the rain falls over the town,
and he thinks he might tease
the cottonwool fluff into strands
of thin mist, and blank everything out,
and he thinks he might blow
this dandelion clock so high,
it will never come down, and he thinks
he might eat it, a taste of marshmallow
sliding inside him, filling him up
with emptiness, till he's all space,
and he thinks, when he's hollow and full,
he might float away.

LADY FRANKLIN'S MAN

"I can never be a happy person, because I live too much in others."
– Lady Jane Franklin

I
Lady Franklin Recalls a Flag

1845

A few days before you sailed,
we were sitting up
after dark. We fell quiet; I think
you were almost asleep,

and I was stitching your flag
by the light from the fire.
You'd had a chill: I looked up
and saw you shiver,

and a tenderness shook me all through.
I knelt on the mat
and draped the flag over your knees
to keep the cold out.

And you started, wide-eyed: "Don't you know
only a dead man
has *that* thrown over him?"
You looked so drawn,

so shaky, your face of a sudden
grey, and I thought: *how long
since those lines came; how many years
has he not been young?*

II
Lady Franklin Begins to be Concerned

1847

When first you sailed, all my pictures of you
were bright. I could fancy all your lines
smoothing away in the wind, the northern light
you love so well.

That stiffness in your shoulder would start to ease
with action; even the headaches would fade,
as the hate-filled faces of Hobart
fell back in your wake.

And you would go forward, west until west
became east, until nameless channels
became safe passage, until a private man,
a man who shunned fame,

a man who'd blow a fly off his hand
rather than kill it, became a hero.
The man I love. I have always known
it was there in you,

under the gentleness. People forget,
seeing you at a desk or in an armchair,
what an adventurer you were. The man
who ate his boots,

who starved and lived... I was glad of your sailing,
that May morning, a white dove at your mast,
knowing you'd come back whole, healed, yourself
as you were meant to be.

But now the third winter is drawing down,
and no sign. Are you iced-in
up there, like Ross, watching the sun set,
knowing it won't rise

for months? Those men came back with a taste
for seal-fat, speaking little, afraid of the dark,
sharing no memories. Who will you be
when you come home?

III
Lady Franklin at Muckle Flugga

1849

I suppose you must have passed this place
as you sailed north: the last lighthouse
in the kingdom. I can hear you saying
– if this letter reaches you at all –
"Whatever is she doing up there?"
Well, I came to the northern isles
to meet the whalers on their way home
from Greenland. I thought I might find one
who'd seen you, had news of you.

I know now that they haven't. They are kind,
so kind, but they can tell me nothing.
I could have gone home weeks ago
but I stayed in Lerwick, sending letters
by every northbound captain – I wonder
if you ever saw one?

                    Up here, they have
a different sky – well, you knew that,
but I did not. I could hardly believe it
after London: this high, vast vault
with three levels of cloud, and the air
pure enough to drink... I knew
it must be this sky you were seeing,
and it felt so clear, as if I could call
to you and be heard over any distance,
as if I could reach into the deep blue
and touch you.

                    That was why
I came here, I think, farther north still,
to the last lighthouse. I wanted to be
a few miles closer, as if it could help.

Mr Edmondston understood: he is a good man.
He showed me the little rock, the Out Stack,
beyond here, even, the northernmost point
on our soil. I looked so long, and he knew
my mind, and rowed me there.

                                So I stood
where I think few ever went, or wanted to,
southwards a whole country at my back
and northwards – what? Ocean, sky, nothing
to break or change them. The nothing,
the emptiness, you sailed into.

It is night now, but not dark:
these are the blue summer nights
you told me of, and I am writing this
by a window at the Edmondstons'
without lamp or candle. It will sail
with some captain, perhaps to find you,
perhaps not. But today on that rock
I was so close to you, I knew
we could not be closer in a bed.

IV
Lady Franklin Refuses to Wear Mourning

1851

Eleanor, please don't think ill of me.
Do you suppose I like wearing pink

at my age? I never liked it much
– a sickly colour. And as for this bright green...

But it shouts to all and sundry: *I believe*
he is alive. Unless I show that,

they'll give him up for lost. I need them
to pester *The Times*, sign petitions,

write cheques, make speeches. Men have lived
years out there. They *must* go on searching,

and they will, if I keep them in mind
of him. The legend, the traveller

in hard places, the hero in the ice:
he has to live for them. The right words,

acts, gestures, dress, could bring him back,
as sure as magic, but if I make

one mistake, the spell will not work:
you know how it is in stories.

It must be the right lamp, the right lips
kissing the sleeper, the right words exactly,

or the door stays closed. The door
to men's hearts, to the Admiralty's purse,

to the ice, to him. Who will conjure it open
if not me, in my mountebank's cloak?

V
Lady Franklin and the Kindness of Strangers
1853

Little adventurer, I am sorry.
I have been all night crying for you,

my poor René. That the ice should take
one so warm-hearted. You were too young,

I should never have let you risk your life,
and twice, at that. You were hardly home

before you shipped again, for a man
you had never seen. What kindness I find

in men. Mr Kennedy leaves his business
to look after itself in Canada.

Dr Kane, who knows he will not live
to see forty, takes his weak heart north,

when he might rest in comfort. Even Ross –
impossible man, but when I think

how he sailed, so old, on such a journey....
And you, my dear, come from your home in France

in such haste, who loved dancing and laughter,
to die in a cold sea. Edward told me

the crew wept for you: he could barely speak
himself. I told him he, at least,

must not go north a third time: I would see
no more young lives lost. He just looked

from under those dark brows of his:
"I would go out again. *He* would have, too."

I wonder if so many men have gone
questing like this, since Arthur reigned a king,

if he ever did. A kind man draws
kindness from others: a brave man

helps them find courage. Up there, they say,
under the ice, in the dark of the dead winter,

lies the magnetic pole that attracts all
the shivering needles northward.

VI
Lady Franklin Hears a Ballad in the Street

1857

I heard that song again today.
The coalman whistling on his cart
left his breath on the frosty air
and the notes sparkled down our street

to a young girl scrubbing her step.
Ten thousand pounds I would gladly give,
she crooned... A shop-lad took it up:
... to know on earth Lord Franklin lives.

And, as ever, the word jars.
He is no lord, I want to call:
just plain Sir John... I bite it back.
I am too glad to hear your tale

still on their lips, your name spoken,
to quarrel with a misplaced word.
I can guess why they call you so:
where there's a Lady, there's a Lord,

so they must think. It is my fault:
knowing my name, they change yours,
and I am known. I am the one
who makes the speeches, writes the letters:

you are unseen behind the ice,
oceans and years away, a man
of story, an adventurer's quest.
Some child will ask me, now and then,

if you are real or "just in books".
Your name has floated free of you,
a phrase of song upon the air.
All down the street, I hear your echo.

VII
Lady Franklin Receives News

1859

I did not think you could have left the world,
and I not know it. I thought I would feel your death
like a lack of warmth or food: I am cold, I am hungry,
I am a widow. I thought it would be like that.

June the eleventh, eighteen-forty-seven...
I had to look back in my diaries
to know what kind of a day that was,
the day a gap closed up where you had stood,

and I find it was like any Friday.
I left my card, answered a few letters,
wondered if you were on your way back.
I hadn't even started to worry.

And you were dying – of what? I wish the note
had said. An accident, an illness?
At least, then, most of your officers
were still alive. I hope they were with you.

I hope someone, Crozier or Fitzjames,
held you in his arms. I hope someone
spoke to you, told you *I'm here*, all through.
I hope you never felt alone.

All the time I was raising money,
fitting out ships, begging the Admiralty
to send more men in search, you were not there.
When I stood on the rock and felt you close,

on the empty ocean, you were not there.
When poor René Bellot gave his life,
when street-lads sang your ballad, when *The Times*
said every boy in Britain knew your name,

you were nowhere. Or in the boys' mouths,
in the ballad, in the minds of men
like René, Edward, William Kennedy,
Captain M'Clintock.... I should like to think

they went because you were somewhere,
not nowhere, that you drew them north.
René told me he knew no class or nation
up there: that all men were his brothers.

Perhaps you – *that* you – are still somewhere,
the you who made that happen. The man
who'll have a statue, a plaque in the Abbey,
a place in story. That man won't die,

but I am thinking now of the man
who hated to see anyone hurt,
whose toes were always cold, who liked his tea
so much. That man will be in no ballads:

I am not sure anyone would believe
in him now, but I knew him, and he died
on June the eleventh, eighteen-forty-seven,
and whoever was near him, I was not.

VIII
Lady Franklin Resumes her Travels
1860-69

New York

Loud voices, brash ways,
with kind hearts. You would like them,
if you could know them.

Brazil

Cruel. Bright. Poor folk
at the rich men's carnival.
Hobart with music.

Patagonia

Wind blowing over
an empty land: who would choose
that sound to die to?

California

They are still digging
for gold here: may all men find
what they most search for.

British Columbia

Canoes took us up
the Fraser, Indian-paddled,
like you, long ago.

Hawaii

Girls, mission-dressed, eyes
cast down, hands and feet tracing
forbidden dances.

Japan

The locked land opened
to your name: I was honoured
to carry it there.

Singapore

Straight streets, prim manners.
Who travelled so far, to make
the place they came from?

Suez

Cranes and great dredgers
sucking sea, shaping land; what
can hinder men now?

Dalmatia	Harsh coast, fishermen who feed all strangers. I hope you met men like these.
Germany	The view took my breath, but I went up by litter. Age: the worst mountain.
France	The Exhibition: the world's eyes on this city. René should be here.
India	Ten feet up, swaying, feeling sick, on this grey deck, this elephant-ship.
N.W. Africa	Dark archways lengthen, tempt. The best road is risky, the best place unknown.

IX
Lady Franklin Fails to Write an Epitaph

1875

Words fail me, they say.... When I needed
to persuade, I could make words serve me:

that is why your monument is building
in the Abbey. Your name where it belongs,

in stone, in glory. It is what I wanted
for you. Yet now, given the chance

to write words for it, I cannot.
Four lines to say what you were:

I have written twelve-page letters
telling the world that, and now

I can shape nothing. You'd laugh:
you were the shy, the tongue-tied one.

The Laureate is writing it – I think
he calls you "heroic sailor-soul",

but to me he is always the lad
who annoyed you, all those years ago,

by putting his feet on the furniture –
not that you said. You left words to me,

but words have left me, now. I feel tired,
these days. I walk with a staff,

like some old wizard, but I make
no magic. Perhaps my spirits are gone

at last. The words must be right,
exactly right, or things will not happen....

Notes to Lady Franklin's Man

In 1845 Sir John Franklin, aged 59, led an expedition to the Arctic to complete the North-West Passage. When, after two years, he had not returned, the Admiralty began a massive search. By the early 1850s, with little found, they were ready to abandon it. Lady Franklin, conscious that men from earlier expeditions had survived years in the Arctic, opposed this. She financed ships herself and persuaded others to, but to do this, and to keep the Admiralty searching, she needed public opinion on her side, which she gained by cultivating Franklin's image as an Arctic hero.

Lady Franklin Begins to be Concerned
"Hobart" Not long before, Franklin had been a most unhappy governor of Tasmania. He and Lady Franklin had, by trying to improve the lot of the convict and aborigine inhabitants, attracted the hostile contempt of the British expatriates who made up Hobart society. The appointment ended early: Franklin returned to England close to nervous exhaustion and, so he thought, with his reputation damaged. That was why he agreed to go north.

"Ross" Sir John Ross, some years earlier, had been trapped four years in Arctic ice but brought home 19 of his 22 men alive and fairly well.

Lady Franklin at Muckle Flugga
"Mr Edmondston" Keeper, at the time, of the Muckle Flugga light off Shetland.

Lady Franklin Refuses to Wear Mourning
"Eleanor" Franklin's daugher by his first wife.

Lady Franklin and the Kindness of Strangers
"René" Lt. Joseph-René Bellot of the French navy, who had obtained leave to go searching for Franklin at his own expense. He was 27, endearingly affectionate, and Lady Franklin treated him as a son.

"so old" The Admiralty refused to send Sir John Ross (q.v.) to search for Franklin, on the ground that he was 73. He went anyway, financing his own ship and running up debts of £500, because he'd given Franklin his word that he would.

"Edward" Commander Edward Inglefield, on loan from the Navy to one of Lady Franklin's expeditions. He, like Bellot, had been out twice for her and refused her offers of pay.

Lady Franklin Receives News
In 1859 Captain Leopold M'Clintock returned from yet another search financed by Lady Franklin, (the Admiralty had bowed out by then), with evidence of the expedition's fate, including a note found in a cairn which confirmed that Franklin had died in 1847.

Lady Franklin Resumes her Travels
Lady Franklin was a great traveller all her life; this itinerary from one decade is, believe it or not, selective.

Lady Franklin Fails to Write an Epitaph
"The Laureate" Tennyson, Franklin's nephew by marriage, came up with:

Not here! the white north has thy bones; and thou,
Heroic sailor-soul,
Art passing on thine happier voyage now
Toward no earthly pole.

One can only wish Lady Franklin had trusted herself to do the job. She died, aged 83, before the monument was completed, which gave the Dean of Westminster the chance to add a few lines commemorating her. His prose put Tennyson's verse to shame:

"...this monument was erected by Jane, his widow, who, after long waiting, and sending many in search of him, herself departed to seek and to find him in the realms of light."

Survivor

Forty-five years ago
you didn't die: you were famous
for staying alive.

You were sixteen.
On Pathé, black hair rumpled
against a white stretcher,

you looked like Elvis.
Whatever you'd done, whatever
the witless bravado,

the violence, your eyes
gazed wide and dark. Bone structure
to die for.

You were beautiful
the way a young man is sometimes
for a few years,

no more. That transience
glows through the skin, says *Now,*
take it now,

there's no tomorrow.
Nor there was, I know, for the man
you killed, nor the man

who died for you –
I'm not forgetting. But when
I see the shots

of you now: the paunch,
the grey hair thinning, the skin
dulled and slackened

with sixty-one years,
it seems there is death, and death,
and against my will

my mind does not run
on the brave nor the innocent.
I am mourning

your moment long gone,
your worthless, ephemeral face
that coarsened quickly

in some prison;
that would have coarsened slowly
in any case.

Lockerbie Butter

Scottish hotels serve it in small wrapped portions,
to go with plastic thimblefuls of jam
or marmalade, and no-one bats an eyelid.
I did see someone, once, notice the name

and blench, and I thought he might ask
"Say, is that the place where the plane fell
out of the sky?" But he didn't; he spread it
on his toast, went on as usual,

as people do. A plane, miles above,
is blown apart, gouges a burning crater
where, just lately, folk were going about
their lives, seeing to some daily matter,

when all their days were torn in one handful
out of the calendar. And what was once
a name on a station, a map, a packet,
comes to mean murder, grief, cosmic mischance.

At first its people stumble through the wreck
of logic, dazed, asking *why us?*
By and by, being marked out for sorrow
turns to comfort. They put on grace, conscious

of cameras, strangers, the eyes of the dead:
they live on levels where they had not known
they could breathe. Soon the press-pack will tire
of heroes; write *Feud in Tragedy Town*,

then move out, leaving them to go back
to normal. Yet even in the first days,
while the great scar still throbbed, while fields bore
children's belongings, while widows hugged space,

some folk were out milking incurious cows,
which pause no more for grief than does the sun.
Milk comes twice a day and spoils quickly
if not attended to; things go on,

and someone told me once how he froze,
(on holiday, just wandering around),
to see musicians play some pretty waltz
under their banner: Dachau Town Band.

Well, they could change the name... but if a name
could make it not the place of death, why then
it wouldn't be the place of birth either,
their birth, I mean, nor that of any man

who ever led a decent life there,
whose word was good, who was a careful father
or a kind son, who spoke against wrong,
who made others long to live better.

A meadow pastures cattle: soldiers come
and soak it red, lime it with their youth,
and by and by, as dust and distance take them,
the flattened grass rises in their path,

and it grows from bones and grief and courage
and agony: the dead are in each blade,
and they are not diminished nor forgotten
in its unfailing greenness: all they did

and felt and suffered is in memory,
in the neighbourhood, the ground, the town,
in daffodils blazing round the Clifford tower,
in the children of Dunblane, Aberfan,

in every note of music played in Dachau
and in these oblongs: death turned to grass,
grass turned to milk, milk turned to a living,
the small gold ingots of the commonplace.

The Stout Centurion

It fills its glass case,
circling a waist long gone,
the soldier's belt.

Not for war,
this wide front encrusted
with gold. Parade wear:

heavy, impressive.
The visitors admire,
pass on.

The back can't detain
them long: plain leather.
Nothing to see

but holes: five round,
the sixth, beyond them,
stretched to an oval,

and beyond that, one,
not punched by a craftsman,
but jabbed in

with a blade. His blade.
I can see him
so clearly, standing

hours under the sun
and this weight, gold edges
biting into folds

of flesh, raising
red weals. He's feeling sick
and his ribs ache,

and he isn't thinking
of eagle or Empire
or anything else

except the moment
he can suck in, unbuckle,
let it all go.

Night Nurses in the Morning

No bench in the bus shelter; they slump
against caving perspex, dragging the Silk Cut

deep into their lungs, eyes closed, holding
the moment, then letting a long breath go.

And they don't talk. Swollen ankles above
big white boat-shoes, dreams of foot-spas.

Pale pink pale green pale blue, even without
the washed-out uniforms you could tell them

from us other early-morning faces
going in, starting the day. We eye them sideways

as they fall into seats, ease their shoes off.
More pallid than colliers or snooker players,

the vampires of mercy. All their haunts lie near
this bus route: here's St Stephen's Hospice,

where folk go to die, there, the Lennox Home
for Elderly Ladies. Just round the bend,

the other granny-park, where I walked past
an open window one evening when the lilac

was out, and heard a young voice scream, over and over,
You bitch, you bitch, and another tone,

querulous and high, a complaining descant
to her theme. They both sounded desperate.

People who live by night aren't quite canny.
We let them keep things running, avoid their eyes,

resenting the way they don't seem to need us there.
What do you do, in the corners of darkness

where we sweep the inconvenient? What is it
you never say to each other on the bus?

As our faces wake, exhaustion silvers
the backs of their eyes: not windows but mirrors.

The Pursuit of Happiness

"... certain unalienable rights... among these are life,
liberty and the pursuit of happiness"
Thomas Jefferson: The American Declaration of Independence, 1776

But he only said
you had a right to chase it:
he never mentioned

catching it up.
Like that coyote,
forever in pursuit

of the road-runner,
forever unpacking
the latest gadget

from Acme, sure
it'll work, this time,
you walk, unerring,

off cliff edges,
into tunnels that echo
with oncoming trains.

The gun backfires; the fuse
is a simmering dud,
till you pick it up.

All feet but yours
escape the traps.
You wait, exactly

where the rock will fall,
watching, far off,
the dust of your dreams:

then it's back
to the Sears & Roebuck
for another miracle.

And if you caught it,
if you ever did,
wouldn't it taste stringy,

all muscle and disappointment,
and what would you do
with the rest of your life?

Partitioning the Hall

*"The summer after Svein's death, his sons put up partition
walls in his great drinking-hall."* – Orkneyinga Saga

Well, when would either of us give a banquet
for eighty people? Now I think of it,
I don't *know* eighty people. I remember
shrivelling against the wall, last summer,
as he laughed and clowned and pledged each man
in the hall by name, while the Earl looked on,
his face darkening. Yet he loved him, too,
from a safe distance. I can hear him now:
"Svein, old friend, you're getting no younger.
You have to go raiding twice a year,
risking your life, to pay for all this,
and is it worth it, if one of these days
your luck runs out? Stay home, settle down:
a quiet life's better than a high one."
And the old man grinned. "Honest, just one more,
one raid this autumn, and it's all over."

When we were little, he'd be telling us stories
late at night, and mother would say: "Those boys
should be in bed", and he'd plead: "Just one more".
We loved them: revenge, escape, murder,
our dreams all blood and guts...
                                        "So I came back
from the fishing, and found our house burned black,
the thatch gone and a taste of smoke in my throat,
and your granddad in the ashes, caught like a rat
in a trap.... I knew the bastard's name
who'd done it, all right: later I torched his farm."

I wonder if this wood will last out?
It's a hell of a big job.... Be well worth it,
though: two normal rooms instead
of that great barn where you couldn't be heard
without shouting through your hands. I missed
his voice so much, at the funeral feast:

he could make it carry over a storm
or a battle, never mind a room,
and sometimes I thought it too loud,
until it wasn't there.
                    He'd have enjoyed
the feast: all those old men swapping stories
from Earl Rognvald's time: those were the days...
fighting in Caithness... remember when...
that raid on Wales... in exile... me and Svein....
It was strange; like listening to legend
or history. It's hard to understand
how troubled those times used to be.

There'll be no revenge; no mad journey
to raze Dublin. Even if we could,
what for? He died on a Viking raid,
robbing their goods; they did what they had to.
Oh, if I saw them; if they stood here now,
if someone claimed the honour: *I'm the one*
who killed Svein Asleifarson,
I'd bury my axe haft-deep in his head.
No sense in it, though. Those days are ended,
blood-feuds, autumn-raids, revenge killing,
no room for all that.
                    I can't stop thinking
how he died in that pit, like a bloody trapped bear,
looking up at their weapons. The world grew smaller
around him. But it'll do for me.
I'm a farmer; I don't want to be
a saga-hero or rival the Earl,
or feast eighty men in my hall.
I want to get by in quiet times,
stay out of trouble, have peaceful dreams
and die of old age
                    ... though that's the bit
that scares me to hell, I'll admit.
Helpless in a bed, looking this way and that,
a ring of kind faces and no way out....

Easter

Outside the library
the old drinkers rock
and hug themselves,

crying softly, cursing,
and the snow falls
in slow motion

through the bloom
of a flowering cherry.
April showers.

A man stumbles
on his wavy line
across ground that glitters,

his tread crunching
snow crystals, broken glass
and white petals

that bruise to a faint
pink smear behind him,
as if he walked barefoot.

The Extra

I forget which film
(black and white, thirties)
has a crowd scene,

a liner leaving port,
and among the extras
at the ship's rail

stands an old man
with a rather distinctive hat
and a wistful face,

waving his farewells
to the extras on shore,
among whom,

with a rather distinctive hat,
by some continuity cock-up
he also stands.

I hope the director
didn't give him hell
for wrecking the shot,

because no moment
has moved me more.
So many voyagers

since the world began,
leaving one self, one country,
one life, for another,

and never a man
embarks, without looking back
at what stays behind:

the face, translucent
as a sloughed snakeskin,
the thin figure,

fading at the edges,
who raises a hand
slowly, in a gesture

that aches in the bones
all the way
to the other side.

Toast

When I'm old, I'll say *the summer*
they built the stadium. And I won't mean

the council. I'll be hugging the memory
of how, open to sun and the judgement

of passing eyes, young builders lay
golden and melting on hot pavements,

the toast of Cardiff. Each blessed lunchtime
Westgate Street, St John's, the Hayes

were lined with fit bodies; forget
the jokes, these jeans were fuzz stretched tight

over unripe peaches. Sex objects,
and happily up for it. When women

sauntered by, whistling, they'd bask
in warm smiles, browning slowly, loving

the light. Sometimes they'd clock men
looking them over. It made no odds;

they never got mad; it was too heady
being young and fancied and in the sun.

They're gone now, all we have left of them
this vast concrete-and-glass mother-ship

that seems to have landed awkwardly
in our midst. And Westgate's dark

with November rain, but different, as if
the stones retain heat, secret impressions

of shoulder-blades, shallow cups,
as sand would do. The grey façade

of the empty auction house, three storeys
of boarded windows, doesn't look sad,

more like it's closed its eyes, breathing in
the smell of sweat, sunblock, confidence.

The Truth

Again and again, I have conjured you both
for nothing. To think an island
I never saw, in St Julian's Bay,
a trial, a death sentence, two men:
that's easy. But when the play goes on,

I lose the plot. Accuser and condemned
kneeling on deck to take the bread and wine,
rising in tears. Dining together, laughing,
at ease, drinking each to the other's voyage
– one round the world, one out of it.

And then you go back to the island,
where the block waits, and you walk apart
from all watchers, a little way
along the beach, and the words you speak,
no-one will ever know. You embrace

in plain sight: the one marked for death
prays aloud, but what lies behind
word and act? I need to move inside
your minds: it's my trade, and the way
is as mazy as Magellan's Strait.

What do I know of you? Both arrogant,
stubborn, devout: one choleric, one cool.
Even so much comes from men's words
who colour you their way, as I must.
Write what you see, they say, trust the reader.

Can it be enough to write the Host
on your tongues, the tracks of tears, kind words
over wine, a walk in sight of the block,
lips making unheard shapes, a farewell?
Perhaps. But all the maker in me

wants more, wants to know it's you
as you were, not some mountebank's illusion.
I want a scrap of paper, a proof:
did the admiral never, in his cups,
speak out of turn to some captured Spaniard

who kept journals: would a gentleman-adventurer
show up on some deep statesman's payroll?
Sometimes I think if I could only walk
on the island, listen to the silence,
I would hear, still whispering in surf,

hanging in the air, the words you spoke,
like the faintest hint of spice on the wind,
like the perishable truth, that so seldom
survives its voyage home. I listen close.
Again and again, you walk out of earshot.

Acknowledgements

Some of these poems have previously appeared in: *Acumen*, *The Bridport Prize Anthology 1999*, *The Exeter Poetry Prize Anthology 1999*, *Fine Lines* (BBC Radio 4), *Interchange*, *The Peterloo Prize Anthology 2000*, *Poetry Ireland*, *Poetry Review*, *Poetry Wales*, *Seam*, *Stand*, *Thumbscrew*, *The Times Literary Supplement* and *The Yellow Crane*.

Also by Sheenagh Pugh

Poetry
Beware Falling Tortoises
Id's Hospit
Prisoners of Transience
Selected Poems
Sing for the Taxman
Stonelight

Fiction
Folk Music